ATLANTA FULTON PUBLIC LIBRARY

P9-EMM-863

P9-EMM-863

SWAN LAKE

AS TOLD BY

MARGOT·FONTEYN

AND ILLUSTRATED BY

Trina Schart Hyman

GULLIVER BOOKS

HARCOURT BRACE JOVANOVICH

San Diego   New York   London

J792.842
Fonteyn

Text copyright © 1989 by Margot Fonteyn

Illustrations copyright © 1989 by Trina Schart Hyman

All rights reserved. No part of this publication
may be reproduced or transmitted in any form or
by any means, electronic or mechanical, including
photocopy, recording, or any information storage
and retrieval system, without permission in
writing from the publisher.

Requests for permission to make copies of any
part of the work should be mailed to:
Permissions, Harcourt Brace Jovanovich, Publishers,
Orlando, Florida 32887.

Library of Congress Cataloging-in-Publication Data

Fonteyn, Margot, Dame, 1919–

Swan lake.

"Gulliver books."

Summary: A prince's love for a swan queen overcomes an
evil sorcerer's spell in this fairy-tale adaptation of
the classic ballet.

[1. Ballets—Stories, plots, etc. 2. Fairy tales] I. Hyman, Trina Schart, ill.
II. Tchaikovsky, Peter Ilich, 1840–1893. Lebedinoe ozero. III. Title.

PZ8.F668Sw   1989   [Fic]   87-7573

ISBN 0-15-200600-1

C D E

HBJ

The illustrations in this book were done in india ink, acrylic,
and pastel on Bainbridge board.
The display type was hand-lettered by the artist.
The text type was set in Berkeley Old Style by
Thompson Type, San Diego, California.
Printed and bound by Tien Wah Press, Singapore
Production supervision by Warren Wallerstein
and Rebecca Miller
Designed by Joy Chu

ACHB

To Dame Alicia Markova,
the most ethereal of ballerinas,
my first Swan Queen, my first Giselle,
my idol and greatest inspiration

—M.F.—

For Michael O'Donnell,
with love.

—T.S.H.—

LONG AGO, there was a prince named Siegfried. He lived in a castle perched high on a mountain, with views for miles around. Pine forests stretched down the mountain slopes to a great, dark lake, which was lost in white mists in the early morning.

Prince Siegfried's father was dead. His mother, the Princess, was ruling the land until the time when Siegfried came of age. Wishing to raise him to be serious and responsible, she engaged a wise old man to be his tutor. But whenever he was free from his studies, Siegfried joined his friends in singing, dancing, and drinking the good country wines.

More than anything, he loved to go hunting. As he rode through the endless green forests, Siegfried felt he was in an enchanted world where anything might happen.

The day soon arrived when Siegfried came of age, and a big celebration was held on the castle grounds. Many young people from neighboring villages came to congratulate their prince, for they all loved him. Although he enjoyed the festivities, he was aware that this day marked the end of his carefree years. Because he was born a prince, Siegfried had an air and manner that set him apart from others. Now that he was to be ruler of the land, he would become a little more distant from even his closest friends. The thought made him sad, but he did not allow it to spoil the happiness of his guests as they danced and made merry in the gardens.

Late in the afternoon, the Princess and her ladies-in-waiting were seen approaching from the castle terrace. The jugs of wine were quickly hidden under the tables so she would not see them. And everyone grew very respectful, bowing and curtsying as she passed. Most people—even her ladies-in-waiting—were awed by the Princess. They rarely smiled unless they saw her smiling first.

On this occasion the Princess was in an excellent mood. She loved her son dearly, even though he did not always obey her wishes, and she had chosen a present she knew would delight him. It was a very fine hunting bow.

As soon as Siegfried took the crossbow in his hands, he felt it was important quite beyond its actual value. He kissed his mother's hand most affectionately to thank her.

The Princess smiled—and so, of course, did the ladies-in-waiting. Then she reminded her son that when he came of age, he was expected to marry. Siegfried must choose a bride at the castle ball the very next night.

"Oh, no," Siegfried protested. "I cannot marry yet. It is impossible—there is no one I love."

The Princess's smile vanished. "You know very well it is the ancient custom of our land," she said. "You must perform your duty. The wedding cannot be delayed."

Displeased, she turned to leave without another word. Siegfried bowed deeply in apology, but his mother was not mollified. Nor was any sympathy to be expected from her attendant ladies as they swept after her back to the castle.

As soon as they were out of sight, the wine was put back on the tables and the goblets refilled. The interruption was quickly forgotten by everyone except the Prince.

Evening was falling as the guests began to leave. The Prince was melancholy and preoccupied. No one dared to speak to him until Benno, his closest friend, suggested that a group of them go hunting. Siegfried thought it was a wonderful idea.

"Ah, yes," he replied, "when the moon is high, let us gather by the lake. There I will try my new bow."

HIS FRIENDS SET OFF SOON down the winding path through the pine forest. Siegfried rode slowly behind the others, not wishing to speak with anyone. His mother's words still worried him. How could he expect her to understand something he did not understand himself? For Siegfried believed that somewhere his ideal love existed, a maiden he had never seen and could not describe.

At the base of the mountain, he tethered his horse and continued on foot. He felt strangely uneasy.

By the lake, Benno became excited by a flight of beautiful swans that had just circled overhead, ready to descend, and suggested they stay and wait for them.

But Siegfried wanted to be alone and sent his friends to keep watch farther along the shore.

The swans landed on the water. They swam past him in a long single file, and he was amazed to see that the first swan had a tiny crown on its head. As they came ashore, he aimed his bow.

It was now midnight, and the moon was almost full. In the magical silvery light, the first swan came toward him. He could not believe his eyes. Suddenly standing before him, a swan no longer, was a beautiful young girl shaking flecks of water from her dress as though she were drying her feathers.

Nothing stirred in the silent forest as Siegfried gazed at the pale, shimmering figure. He feared she was an illusion that would melt away at any moment. She had been a swan, he was sure, yet she now had arms and legs and a face more beautiful than any he had ever seen in his dreams.

Unaware of Siegfried, she drew closer to him as he stood spellbound under a tree, scarcely daring to breathe. Her movements were oddly birdlike.

When she saw the Prince the maiden took fright and made as if to fly away, forgetting she no longer had wings. Siegfried quickly laid down his bow and said, "Be not afraid, most gracious maiden, for I will never harm you. I offer you my protection."

She seemed reassured, so he continued. "I have never seen you before, although I come often to the lake. Forgive me if I dare to ask your name."

With dignity she indicated the crown on her head. "I am the Queen of all the swans." She said no more.

"You are a queen and I, Prince Siegfried, bow to you in most respectful homage. But, most gracious Queen, will you permit me to ask how it can be that you are sometimes a swan and sometimes in human form as I see you now?"

She hesitated, wondering whether to entrust her story to this courteous stranger. Finally she said, "Noble Prince, hear my tale, for it is sad indeed. My name is Odette. This lake was created by my mother's tears the day that I and fifty young maidens were turned into swans by an evil magician, who is both man and owl. He allows us to return to human form between midnight and dawn. But he watches over us night and day, so that no one can ever rescue us."

Once again she hesitated. Then, seeing Siegfried's concern, she continued. "There is a way we can be saved from this cruel enchantment. Only if I marry one who pledges his pure and undying love for me alone will the spell be broken. Then we may all return to our families and homes, nevermore condemned to fly above the forests or to swim on the black lake."

As he heard these words, Siegfried realized the meaning of his earlier, unfamiliar emotions, which now overwhelmed him. Falling to his knees before Odette, he declared, "Most beautiful Queen, I never have nor ever will love anyone but you. If you consent to marry me I will be true to you all the days of my life. No one shall ever come between us."

He stood up, one hand on his heart, the other raised high before him, and said, "To this I swear upon all that is most sacred on earth and in heaven."

Odette quivered like a bird. She could find no words, so she gently took his hand in both of hers and pressed it to her heart.

As Siegfried made his pledge, the owl-magician alighted on a rock by the water's edge. Rage distorted his features, but Siegfried was not afraid. He took up his bow and was about to shoot the evil creature, when Odette threw herself between them.

"It is useless," she said. "No mere arrow, not even the finest in the world, has any power against his vile magic. He cannot be destroyed."

She was strong in spirit yet looked so delicate that Siegfried put his arm around her and led her away through the tall trees.

They came upon a clearing, and Odette darted forward as she saw her companions clinging together helplessly, surrounded by the huntsmen with raised bows. When they saw the flight of swans change into beautiful girls before their eyes, the men imagined that some sinister and dangerous hallucination had overcome them. Siegfried arrived just in time to save the terrified maidens from a shower of deadly arrows. He immediately commanded his friends to drop their bows and listen to a story stranger than any hallucination.

Time seemed to stop for the young people as they gathered together in the moonlight. But a sudden chill in the air warned them that dawn was near. Or did the presence of the owl-magician bring about the change? He watched and waited for his captives to turn back into swans as the first rays of daylight touched them.

Siegfried could not bear to let his beloved go. Nor could the Swan Queen bear to leave. They agreed to meet again at midnight. Nothing but the magician's will could have drawn her after her companions as, one by one, they again became swans and swam away.

Siegfried remembered—too late to tell Odette—that he could not return at midnight because he had to attend the castle ball celebrating his birthday. Siegfried tried to shout across the waters, but the unheeding swans vanished silently into the morning mist.

THE GREAT HALL of the castle was vast, with a high vaulted ceiling and windows set in stone walls ten feet thick. Outside, storm clouds obscured the moon. But inside the hall, guests in bright dress glowed in the light of fifty flaring torches.

The Princess, escorted by her son, greeted the assembly, bidding everyone welcome. All who knew Siegfried noticed that he was curiously distant, as though moving in a dream. He paid scant attention to the presentation of the twelve princesses—one of whom he had to choose to be his bride.

All the princesses were beautiful, and each was sure she would be the one the Prince would choose. But as Siegfried danced with them, they began to doubt, for his manner was as cold as a ghost's on a midwinter night.

When the time came for the Princess to ask him which of the lovely young ladies he would marry, Siegfried replied with a curt, "None, madam."

The Princess was shocked and deeply upset, while the would-be fiancées flounced angrily off. The other guests did not know what to do or say.

Just then, new guests were announced and into the hall came a tall man of powerful build and striking appearance, on his arm a beautiful young woman dressed in black. The man presented himself to the Princess as Count von Rothbart and begged leave to present his daughter, Odile. He explained that when news of Prince Siegfried's coming of age had reached their far kingdom, they had started out immediately, hoping to be welcome at the ball.

While he was speaking, the Princess saw that the Count stared straight ahead with unusually round eyes. She also noticed and admired the huge cloak he was wearing but thought his coarse leather gloves quite inappropriate for an evening reception.

Siegfried heard none of the Count's words. He was transfixed by Odile. He went straight to her and gazed into her face.

"You are Odette, my Queen and my true love," he said.

She smiled mysteriously. In her black gown in the torchlit hall, she looked different from the pale figure Siegfried had seen by moonlight. But her face was Odette's—of that he had no doubt.

Von Rothbart (who was of course the owl-magician) had spent the whole day casting a complex and rare spell to alter the face of his daughter to an uncanny likeness of Odette's.

Siegfried did not leave Odile's side for a moment during the rest of the evening. There was so much he wanted to tell her. Her present boldness surprised him compared to her shyness of the night before. But he was also attracted by this new side of Odette, and every minute he fell more in love.

The guests, too, were fascinated by the beautiful stranger—so much so that none of them saw the white swan desperately beating its wings against a window. Only Count von Rothbart and Odile knew the swan was there, and they made sure that Siegfried did not notice it.

Near midnight, Siegfried announced that he had chosen his bride and asked the Princess to bless their engagement. She was overjoyed.

The Count took Siegfried aside and asked him, "Do you truly love my daughter?"

"Yes, I do," replied Siegfried.

"And have you never vowed to love another?" asked the Count.

"Never in my life, nor could I ever do so," said Siegfried.

"You must swear to me on oath that it is so," insisted the Count.

With his left hand on his heart and his right hand upstretched, Siegfried solemnly swore never to love anyone except von Rothbart's daughter.

At once confusion and chaos struck. Lightning zigzagged outside the windows, thunder shook the very walls of the castle, and the torches spluttered and dimmed. In panic the guests ran this way and that.

Siegfried turned toward his fiancée, only to see a hideous parody of Odette's face laughing derisively at him as her father swept her triumphantly away. The Princess fell into a dead faint as she saw an owl's black beak between hooded eyes, and feathers just visible where the Count's ears should have been. An enormous pair of wings escaped from his impressive cloak, and sharp claws from his gloves.

As the couple fled from the hall followed by Siegfried, great flashes of lightning illuminated a white swan piteously flapping its wings at a window. Only then did Siegfried realize that he had been deceived.

In despair he tore outside to reach Odette, but she was gone. He rushed recklessly down the mountain, the bells of the clock tower tolling midnight as he ran.

At the lake he begged the sobbing maidens to tell him where Odette had gone, but they could not speak through their tears. Siegfried collapsed in remorse and misery.

The storm abated, and Siegfried thought he heard the purest of voices calling his name. Lifting his head, he saw Odette walking toward him. She folded her arms around him and raised him to his feet. Their tears mingled in a single stream as they embraced.

The maidens did all they could to shield the lovers from von Rothbart, but he swooped down from the sky to snatch Odette away. Siegfried quickly made the sign of the cross, and the magician lost his hold on Odette. He withdrew to a high, craggy rock to refresh his magic.

"What will become of us now, my beloved?" asked Siegfried.

"Alas, my love, my noble Prince, there is no longer any hope for us. The wicked von Rothbart has used all his cunning to keep me in his power. If I can never be yours in life, I will die rather than live as a swan-maiden. I will throw myself into the lake and remain yours alone for all eternity."

"No, no, stay with me!" he cried. "I love you, and only you. Stay with me, I beseech you!"

Odette embraced him most tenderly, as if to leave her heart and soul in his keeping. Then, quickly slipping out of his arms, she threw herself into the dark waters and was seen no more.

Siegfried hesitated not a moment before following her, and he, too, vanished below the surface at exactly the same spot as his love.

The maidens were deeply distraught, not knowing what would become of them. Some wished to throw themselves into the lake with their Queen; others wanted to escape through the forest while they were still in human form. Still others feared that von Rothbart would put them under even more fiendish enchantments if they defied him.

At that moment von Rothbart, crouched on his rock, began to rise menacingly. Suddenly he stumbled. He stretched out his great wings to prevent a fall, and as he did so, one wing went limp and he rolled over onto his side.

The maidens, huddled together, could see terror in his owl eyes, which had grown enormous. With his good wing, he tried to balance himself, but he did not have enough strength to keep from slipping. Clawing frantically at the rock, he felt the weight of his huge wings dragging him nearer and nearer to the edge. Then he plunged over, crashing to the ground far below. There, thrashing in torment and fury, Count von Rothbart, owl-magician, gave up his life. And at his death, his cruel spells were broken.

For a long time the maidens dared not move, afraid the magician might rise up again more terrifying than before. At last they asked one another cautiously if their captor was really dead.

One maiden, wiser than the others, said, "Dear friends and companions, our Queen and Prince Siegfried overcame the terrible magician by the strength of a love that feared nothing but separation. They are united in happiness forever; for them nothing will ever change. Von Rothbart's powers withered in the face of their love, and we have been released from his evil spell to return to our families and rejoice.

"One day, this lake made by the tears of our Queen's mother will dry up, and the story of our suffering will become a fable. Perhaps it will serve to remind those who hear it that the power of real love is greater than all the forces of evil added together."

STORYTELLER'S NOTE ON THE BALLET

Swan Lake is regarded as one of the great classical ballets. It represents our concern with the eternal conflicts between reality and illusion, truth and deception, good and evil.

The plot is based on a theme recurrent in the legends of many lands, that of a woman who is transformed into a bird. The Stolen Veil, a German version, is thought to have been the inspiration for V. P. Begichev and V. F. Geltser's original production of Swan Lake at the Bolshoi Theatre in Moscow in 1877.

Begichev, director of the Moscow Imperial Theatres, had earlier made a boat trip down the Rhine with the composer Peter Ilyich Tchaikovsky. It is probable that the setting for the ballet was inspired by the striking Rhineland scenery, with its fantastic fairy-tale castles perched high on the bluffs overlooking the river. The story's blend of the human and the supernatural belongs to this nineteenth-century Late Romantic period.

In spite of Tchaikovsky's masterly score, the first production was not a great success, owing mainly to mediocre choreography and to the fact that Tchaikovsky's symphonic mode of composition was new to ballet. Choreographer and dancers complained that much of the music was undanceable, and pieces by lesser composers were substituted or interpolated. Small wonder that Tchaikovsky's friends had strongly advised him against wasting his time writing for ballet! But Tchaikovsky was enthusiastic about composing for the ballet and later wrote two more ballet masterpieces, The Sleeping Beauty and The Nutcracker.

In 1895, eighteen years after the original Moscow production, Marius Petipa, the great French ballet master and choreographer, took up the forgotten Swan Lake music and created his own version at the Maryinsky (now Kirov) Theatre in St. Petersburg. For this production, Petipa revised the plot, reordered some of the music, and delegated the choreography of the swan scenes to his assistant, Lev Ivanov. Ivanov's choreography for the first lakeside scene is still performed almost intact, even though the rest of the ballet has been changed.

The first ballerina to dance Odette-Odile for Petipa was an Italian guest artist of prodigious accomplishment, Pierina Legnani. She came from Milan, then the center of virtuoso training, and was the first to perform the thirty-two consecutive "ronds de jambe fouettés"—turns that climax Odile's dancing in the ball scene.

The part of Prince Siegfried was taken by Pavel Gerdt, the most famous Russian dancer of his time. At age fifty-one, his technique had somewhat diminished—which may explain why Siegfried has only one solo in traditional versions of the ballet.

The complete Swan Lake is given in either three or four acts, comprising four scenes: the celebration in the castle grounds; the first swan scene by the lake; the ball at the castle; and the final lakeside scene.

Frequently the first lakeside scene is performed alone, according to the Ivanov choreography, as "Swan Lake, Act II," and is danced by the two lovers and a corps de ballet of swan-maidens and huntsmen. Siegfried's dances with Odette and Odile are also often presented as excerpts, referred to as "pas de deux from Swan Lake, Act II" (Siegfried and Odette) and "The Black Swan pas de deux" (Siegfried and Odile). The Black Swan pas de deux makes far more sense when seen in the context of the full ballet. Alone it becomes a display of virtuosity with unexplained byplay.

For my own part, having danced Swan Lake many hundreds of times—the two swan acts at sixteen and the full ballet from when I was eighteen—I think one should be aware not only of the duality of the Odette-Odile roles, or good and evil, but also the duality within each role. Both are enigmatic characters; neither is what she seems. Odette is bird as well as woman. Odile is reality as well as illusion.

When I was young, there were one or two more human touches in Odette's scenes. She was a woman with a swan's mannerisms. Now, Swan Queens seem sometimes to forget that point as their interpretations become more "swannish." In consequence, Odette's womanliness is diminished and the dimensions of her duality destroyed.

I always found Swan Lake the greatest challenge in my repertoire and therefore the one that gave me the greatest satisfaction when it went well. The choreography is exacting—the dancers' faults more exposed than in any other ballet. The castle ball scene (Odile's role) requires tremendous stamina. Swan Lake is the only ballet I never felt strong enough to perform twice in the same day.

Swan Lake has a certain mystery that makes each performance of it seem different. It is that mystery— the atmosphere and spirit of the legend—that I have tried to convey in this book.

24 AMMSVILLE - COLLIER HEIGHTS

DISCARDED

DATE DUE

24 COLLIER HEIGHTS

APR 27 1990

J 792.842 FONTEYN   CHB
Fonteyn, Margot
Swan lake

R00254 61108